Meet the Dogs
of
Bedlam Farm

✦ **Jon Katz** ✦

Henry Holt and Company

NEW YORK

For Maria

Henry Holt and Company, LLC
Publishers since 1866
175 Fifth Avenue
New York, New York 10010
mackids.com

Henry Holt® is a registered trademark of Henry Holt
and Company, LLC.
Text and photographs copyright © 2011 by Jon Katz
All rights reserved.

Library of Congress Cataloging-in-Publication Data
Katz, Jon.
Meet the dogs of Bedlam Farm / by Jon Katz. — 1st ed.
p.   cm.
ISBN 978-0-8050-9219-6
1. Working dogs—New York (State)—Juvenile literature.
2. Farm life—New York (State)—West Hebron—Juvenile
literature. 3. Bedlam Farm (West Hebron, N.Y.)—
Juvenile literature. 4. Human-animal relationships—
New York (State)—Juvenile literature. I. Title.
SF428.2.K38 2011
636.7—dc22   2010011698

First Edition—2011
Printed in April 2011 in the United States of America
by Worzalla, Stevens Point, Wisconsin.

10 9 8 7 6 5 4 3

Introduction

Bedlam Farm is in Upstate New York. It is the place where Jon Katz lives and was inspired to write many of his bestselling books about his life and his dogs. He is also a photographer and hospice volunteer. He has kept various animals there, but primarily Bedlam Farm is a place for writing.

This is the story of the four dogs that live on Bedlam Farm.

In the morning after mist has cleared from the path, four dogs go out together for their first walk of the day. They circle and sniff the wet ground carefully, listening and seeing things that only dogs can sense.

The dogs are called

Rose,

Izzy,

Frieda,

and Lenore,

and they all live on Bedlam Farm.

They stay together, circling, never running off. They are a happy group; their tails wag when they see one another. But it wasn't always this way.

Rose, Izzy, and Frieda are working dogs.
They all have jobs to do.

Rose herds sheep.

Izzy visits sick people.

Frieda guards the farm when she's not causing trouble.

Lenore lives on the farm too.
What is *her* job?
Meet the dogs and find out.

❖ Rose ❖

Rose came to the farm when she was six months old. Every day she helps with farm chores. She goes out into the pasture and herds the sheep.

Rose is a border collie.
She is a serious dog,
a smart dog,
a hard-working dog.
She did not always play
or cuddle like Lenore does.

Lenore is different from Rose.
Lenore is carefree and fun-loving.
She would rather eat than work.
She would rather play than chase
sheep. She taught Rose how to play
hide-and-seek, wrestle, and chase
a ball. Now Rose knows how to
have fun too.

Rose helps with farmwork.
Izzy and Frieda are busy too.

What is Lenore's job?

✦ Izzy ✦

Izzy is also a border collie. His story is sad at first. He was abandoned and had lived outside for years. Most of the time, he ran back and forth along a fence. He ran there so much he created a deep trench. It took a long time and lots of love and patience before Izzy learned to be calm and feel safe. But he did.

Now Izzy is a therapy dog
who visits sick people
in their homes,
in hospitals,
and in nursing homes.
He helps people feel better.

Lenore was Izzy's first friend. She chewed on his head, shared her bones, and slept next to him on the floor. She showed him how to live in a house and eat from a bowl. Now Lenore likes to sneak up on Izzy and steal his treats and play tug-of-war.

Every day, Izzy goes off to his job, helping people feel better.
Rose and Frieda are busy too.

But what is Lenore's job?

✦ Frieda ✦

Frieda was a wild dog before coming to Bedlam Farm. She roamed the woods, eating berries and hunting for rabbits, squirrels, and chipmunks.

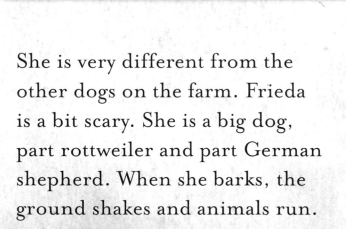

She is very different from the other dogs on the farm. Frieda is a bit scary. She is a big dog, part rottweiler and part German shepherd. When she barks, the ground shakes and animals run.

From the minute she arrived at Bedlam Farm, Frieda started working. She guards the farm. She barks at strangers. She scares off foxes that try to eat the chickens and coyotes that try to eat the sheep.

Sometimes she guards the farm too much and even scares the cats.

Every now and then, Frieda becomes a wild dog again and runs off. Lenore goes out into the woods to find her and bring her back. When Frieda is lonely, Lenore keeps her company and sleeps with her nose-to-nose. Lenore shows her how to be friends with the sheep and other dogs. Lenore shows Frieda how to walk on the path in the woods and leave the squirrels and chipmunks alone.

Even so, Frieda is very busy guarding the farm. She works hard at her job. Rose and Izzy are busy too.

But what *is* Lenore's job?

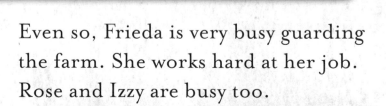

✦ Lenore ✦

Lenore is a black Labrador retriever. She looks for disgusting things to eat, mud to roll in, and people and animals to love. She came to the farm when she was just a puppy.

Lenore is different.
She doesn't guide the sheep, like Rose does.
She doesn't visit people who are sick, like Izzy does.
She doesn't guard the farm, like Frieda does.
She licks the other dogs, touches noses, and wags her tail.

Lenore makes dogs play and people smile.
She makes sure everyone is happy.

Thanks to Lenore, the dogs are a family.
Every night, after they have finished their
work and taken their last walk of the day, they
gather in the warm, cozy farmhouse to eat,
rest, and share the smells, sights, sounds, and
dreams of their busy day with one another.

Rose remembers images of sheep; and Izzy,
the people he helps to feel better; and Frieda,
the many dangers she keeps away.

Lenore does not have work to remember.
But she does have a job.

Lenore is not as quick as Rose, or as busy as Izzy,
or as strong as Frieda. But she is a working dog.

Her job is loving and accepting and having patience.

And that may be the greatest work of all.